The Musician's Notebook

DELUXE EDITION

ISBN 978-0-7624-4800-5

9 8 7 6 5 4 3 2 1
Digit on the right indicates the number of this printing

Cover Illustration © 1998 by Martin Mayo
Designer: Bill Jones
Editor: Greg Jones
Typography: Belucian and Avenir

Running Press Book Publishers
2300 Chestnut Street
Philadelphia, PA 19103-4371

Visit us on the web!
www.runningpress.com

Visit Matt Teacher on the web!
www.sinestudios.com

The Musician's Notebook

DELUXE EDITION

Manuscript paper for inspiration & composition

MATTHEW TEACHER

RUNNING PRESS

PHILADELPHIA • LONDON

Introduction

After more than a decade of helping musicians keep their thoughts, notes, and ideas organized, *The Musician's Notebook* is happy to present this long-awaited Deluxe Edition. We've taken your comments and requests to heart, and as a result you'll find some serious improvements and enhancements that should make it an even more valuable tool for keeping track of your creative moments. *The Musician's Notebook Deluxe Edition* features a larger, more user-friendly hardback format, a special binding that allows the book to lie flat on a music stand while open to any page, and a brand new collection of inspirational quotations from noteworthy figures of past and present.

Writing music can be an elusive process. There are times when inspiration flows faster than notes can be scribbled on a page, while during other periods it can be next to impossible to create anything. There's no predicting when and where the wind will carry a muse to a songwriter's ears, and the result is often illegible lyrics and chord progressions scrawled on whatever's handy when the moment strikes. The notebook you hold is here to help.

In the front of this book you will find a "How To" page that may be used as a key to understanding each element of the composition pages. Each composition page includes two treble staffs (one for melody and one for harmony), a bass staff, tabs for guitar (or use four lines for standard bass guitar), chord boxes, and title and lyric lines. The objective of this unique notebook is to provide an environment for musicians to organize, catalog, transport, and share their original compositions in one streamlined, convenient location.

Another exciting innovation is included in the back of the book: a removable chord chart poster containing major and minor chords for easy reference, plus pages of chord block stickers with the most commonly used chords. The stickers have been formatted to fit right over the printed chord boxes on the composition pages. Should you happen to be using a chord for which there's no sticker, just draw it in by hand.

The power of music is universal and time has proven it to be one of the greatest languages in existence. Make sure you keep track of your inspirations and share them with the world (or at least a friend). As Billy Joel once said, "I think music in itself is healing. It's an explosive expression of humanity. It's something we are all touched by. No matter what culture we're from, everyone loves music."

Musicians may have many positive qualities, but perhaps organization is not one of them. Many songwriters find themselves frantically digging through all their pants pockets searching for some lyric they jotted down earlier only to discover they just cannot locate it. "Was it on the back of that grocery-store receipt? Maybe I wrote it on that parking ticket, or on a random page of one of my mostly empty notebooks? Oh wait, no—I think I might have texted it to myself. . . ." Whatever the case, this notebook is waiting for you to fill it with your songs and keep them safe and orderly for the ages. Hope you enjoy.

—Matt Teacher

You should have high expectations for yourself and others should come second. Making a record is personal, and I really wanted to make something amazing, so I was putting that pressure on myself....

—Florence Welch (b. 1986), Florence and the Machine

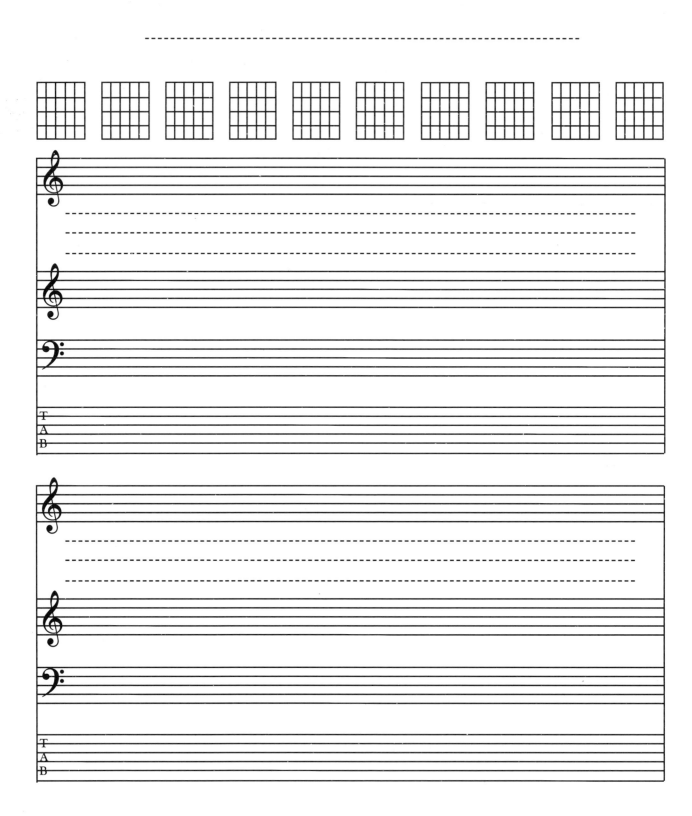

Playing is just about feeling. It isn't necessarily about misery. It isn't about happiness.
It's just about letting yourself feel all those things you already have inside of you but are trying
to push aside because they don't make for polite conversation or something.

—Janis Joplin (1943–1970), American musician

I'm treading a fine line between being really militant with certain views,
and trying to pop it up a little bit so it slips through the cracks.

—Matt Bellamy (b. 1978), Muse

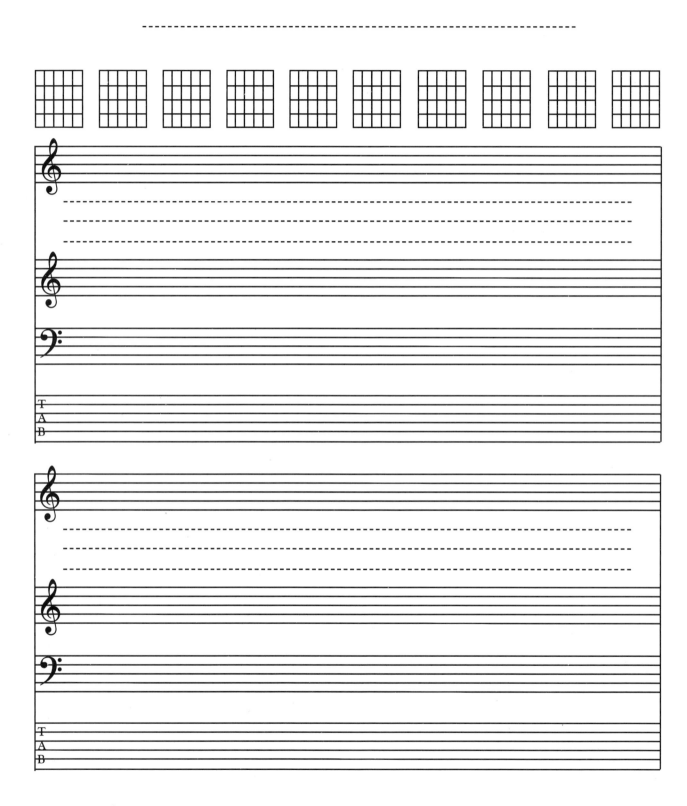

If I were not a physicist, I would probably be a musician. I often think in music.
I live my daydreams in music. I see my life in terms of music.

—Albert Einstein (1879–1955), German physicist

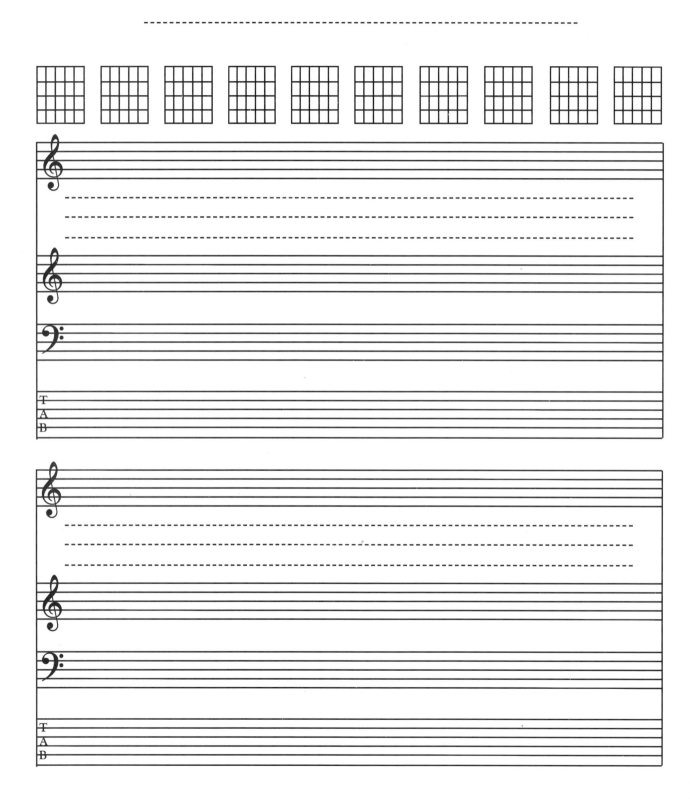

Heartbreak can definitely give you a deeper sensibility for writing songs.
I drew on a lot of heartbreak when I was writing my first album; I didn't mean to, but I just did.

—Adele (b. 1988), English musician

Punk is musical freedom. It's saying, doing and playing what you want. In *Webster's* terms, "nirvana" means freedom from pain, suffering and the external world, and that's pretty close to my definition of punk rock.

—Kurt Cobain (1967–1994), Nirvana

When I have the pressure on me to perform and come up with something very quickly, I can.
I would probably call myself a clutch hitter. I don't like to give myself six months and a million dollars
and a beautiful place to work in. That's not my environment to write.

—Jack White (b.1975), American musician

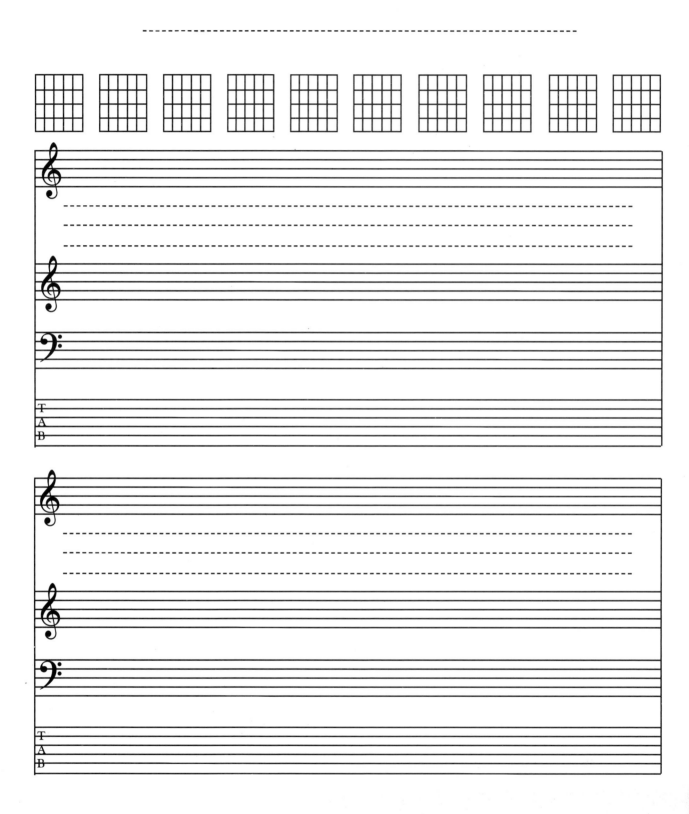

I always try to make the artist feel good because that's the only way I'm going to get the best out of them. The artist is the artist, and you can't be the artist when you're the producer. You've just got to get the best out of them, inspire them, and respect them the way they are.

—RedOne (b. 1972), Moroccan producer; songwriter

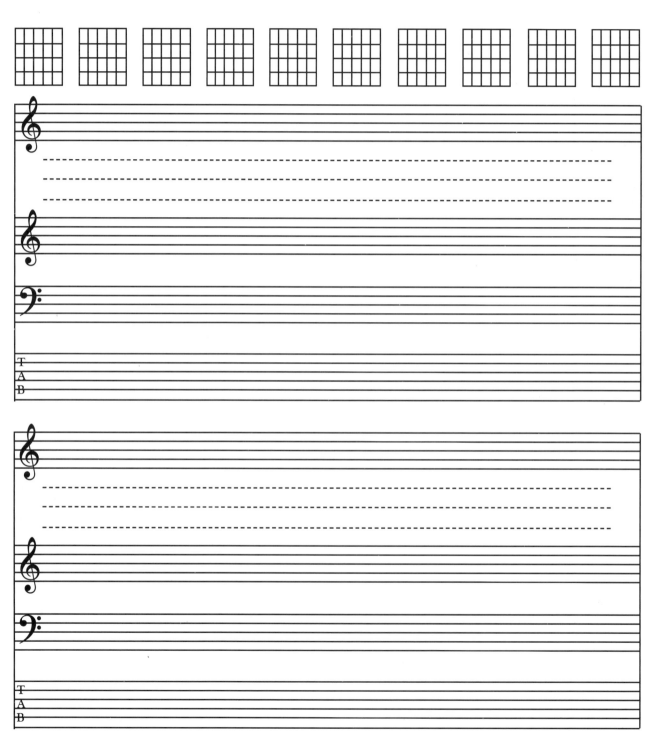

I always enjoyed the feeling of being onstage—the magic that comes. When I hit the stage it's like all of a sudden a magic from somewhere just comes and the spirit just hits you and you just lose control of yourself.

—Michael Jackson (1958–2009), American musician

This is a terrific time to be in a band. Every band has access to the entire world by default. I know quite a few bands that have been able to establish themselves internationally based on nothing other than their web presence. It's an incredible tool.

—Steve Albini (b. 1962), American engineer; musician

Mostly I was just writing about this and that, reading a lot of books, underlining things, remembering what concepts felt like they resonated. I was just on the lookout for what felt like it might go into the sponge and then be able to be squeezed out again.

—Leslie Feist (b. 1976), Canadian musician

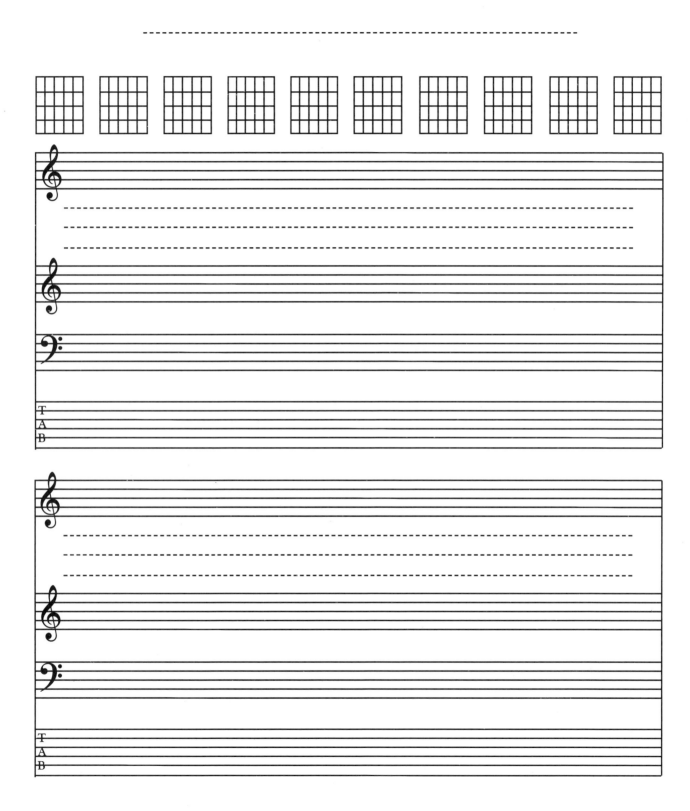

For me, songwriting is something I have to do ritually. I don't just wait for inspiration; I try to write a little bit every day.

—Sean Lennon (b. 1975), American musician

Songwriting is a very mysterious process. It feels like creating something from nothing.
It's something I don't feel like I really control.

—Tracy Chapman (b. 1964), American musician

What I'll do is I'll look for a groove or something to start if off with but then I try to build around it. Try to make something out of it.

—J Dilla (1974–2006), American producer

Marty and Jesse and Neal and I, we learned how to play our instruments together.
We went through that process together, and you can't really replace that. It's a bond for us.

—James Mercer (b. 1970), the Shins

A great song has to make you feel a certain way. Songs can make you happy and sad, they can help you fall in love . . . they have to do something. That's when you get a reaction.

—Leon Huff (b.1942), American songwriter; producer

I have always had a certain song in my head, a certain chemistry of sounds.

—Bjork (b. 1965), Icelandic musician

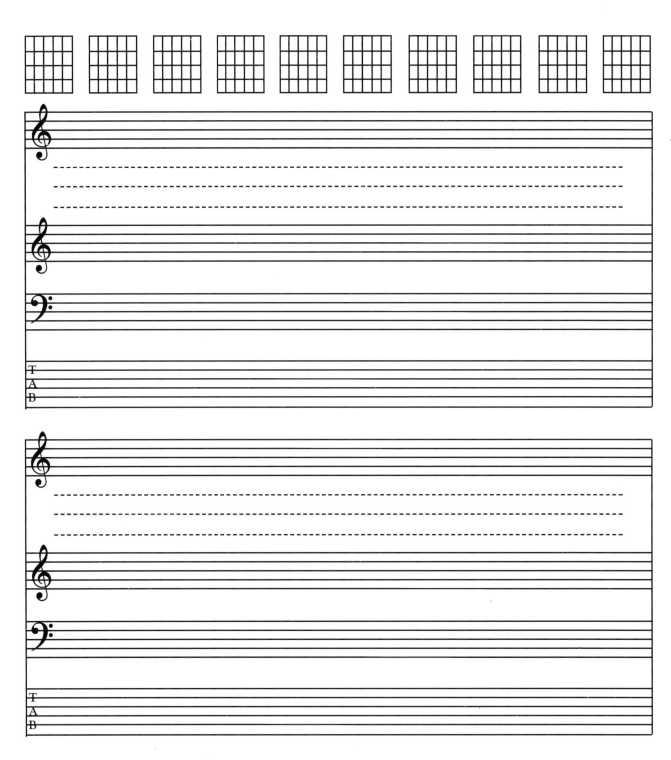

For any aspiring songwriter . . . my advice would be to live life to the fullest, and then write about it.
Dare to suck and put your music out there, and just keep on going.

—Desmond Child (b. 1953), American songwriter; producer

Contrary to what some scary people think, I don't play with a band now for any kind of propaganda-type or commercial-type reasons. It's just that my songs are pictures and the band makes the sound of the pictures.

—Bob Dylan (b. 1941), American musician

There are a lot of people in the band who don't care about being rock stars. We all had backgrounds in activism; we were all interested in social change. It didn't happen right away, but we saw quickly that the music could be used as a tool for change.

—Jesse Walker, Flobots

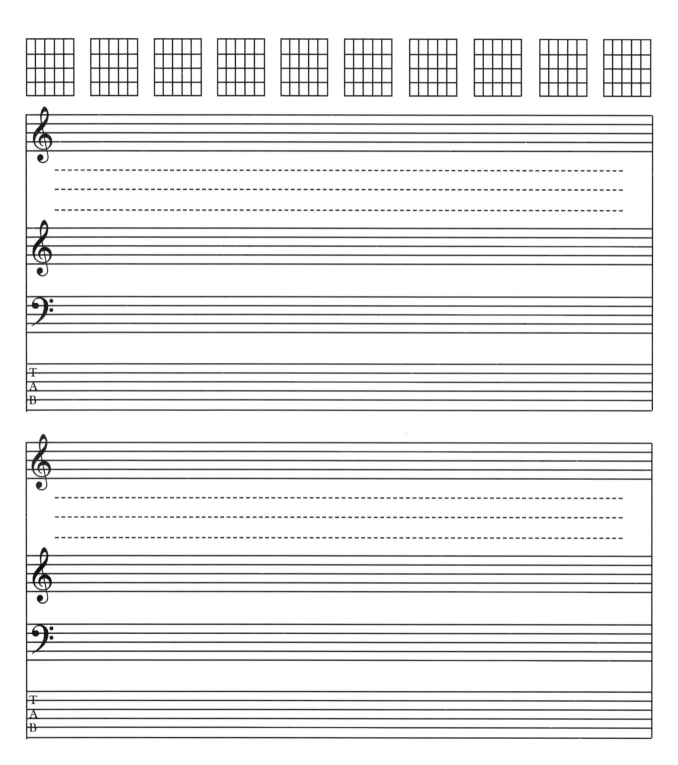

The genre punk itself, for me, it has always been around. It has never gone away and it's becoming —especially in America—a new form of folk music, because there's always a new generation of people who feel that they don't fit in society and people who are skeptical about the world they live in.

—Greg Graffin (b. 1964), Bad Religion

I can rhyme to anything. Just give me a hot beat that everybody's lovin'
and I'll find a flow to it.

—The Notorious B.I.G. (1972–1997), American musician

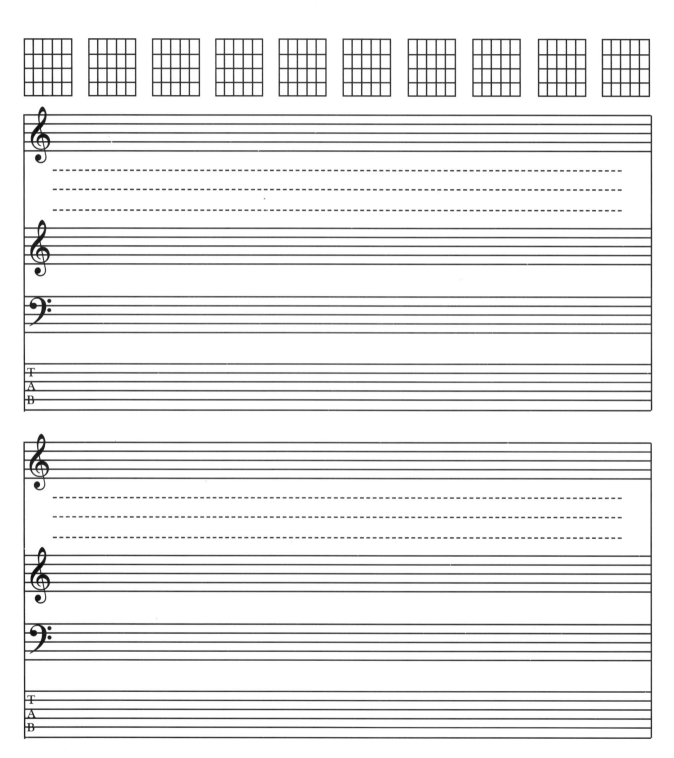

As long as there is truth, there is music.

—Bob Marley (1945–1981), Jamaican musician

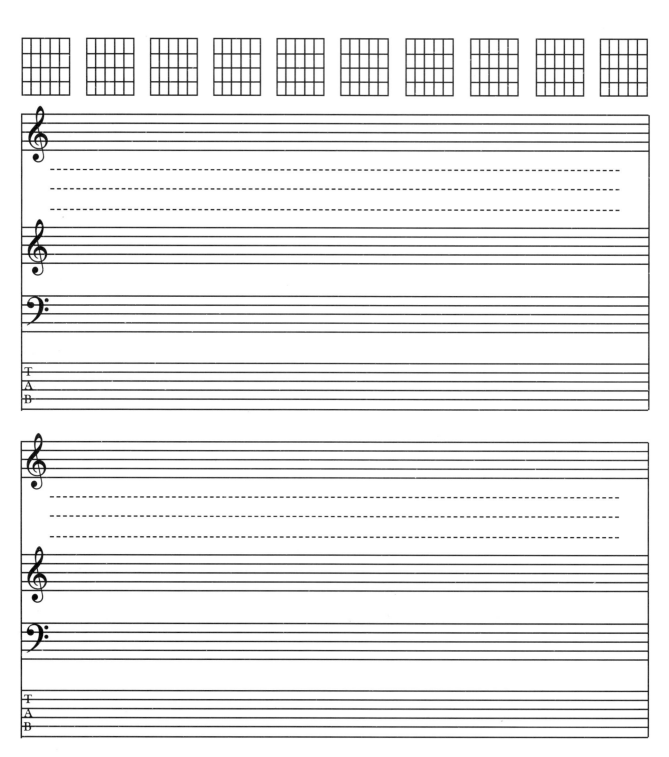

When we're on tour, performance and preparation for performance pretty much preclude writing.
But any other time I'm not on the road, I'm in the studio, working on music.
It hardly feels like a regimen, because it's the greatest joy in the world for me.

—Rivers Cuomo (b. 1970), Weezer

You should take into account when you write a song—it should be fun to play.
When you write a song that's a chore to play, the performances never sound anything but strained.
—Jerry Garcia (1942–1995), the Grateful Dead

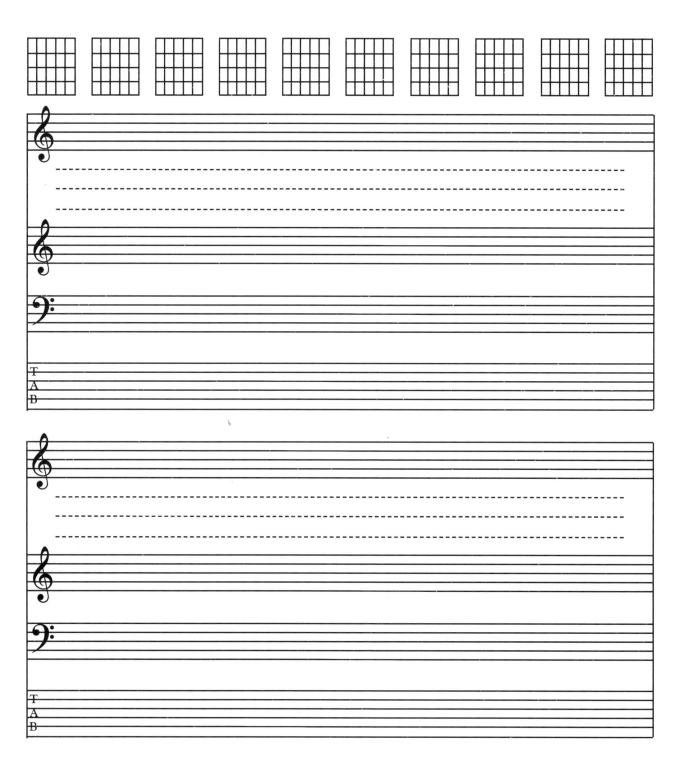

To me, the most powerful records come from a collective creativity.
You get good records when you let all the people who work on it put their personality in their particular area.

—Quincy Jones (b. 1933), American producer

It's tough because you want to make music that reflects your ideals, but considering the isolating process of recording and the time and energy requirements of touring, there aren't a lot of opportunities to express those ideals anywhere but the music itself.

—Robin Pecknold (b. 1986), Fleet Foxes

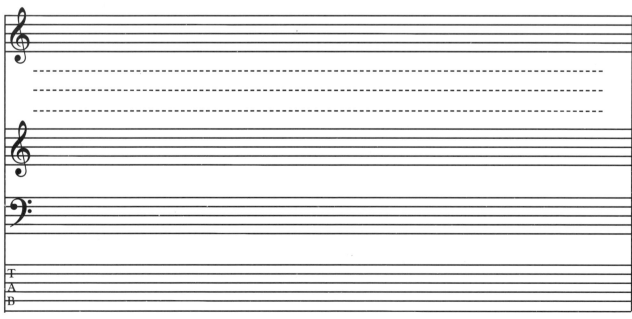

Art is equal parts acceptable and something that you don't understand. It's subject to interpretation and left to the imagination. Simplicity is a law more commonly applied to product, but simplicity can be sophisticated in its own right.

—Cee Lo Green (b. 1974), American musician

I didn't realize I was an exceptional songwriter. I still just kind of think my songs
are like nursery rhymes—little ditties that I write for myself.

—Lily Allen (b. 1985), English musician

Each song has its own secret that's different from another song, and each has its own life. Sometimes it has to be teased out, whereas other times it might come fast. There are no laws about songwriting or producing. It depends on what you're doing, not just who you're doing.

—Mark Knopfler (b. 1949), Dire Straits

This music is not made for us to fight each (other), to kill each other. It's made for us to make people have a good time; it's a universal language of all people. So what I try to push and promote is peace through the whole music industry.

—Snoop Dogg (b. 1971), American musician

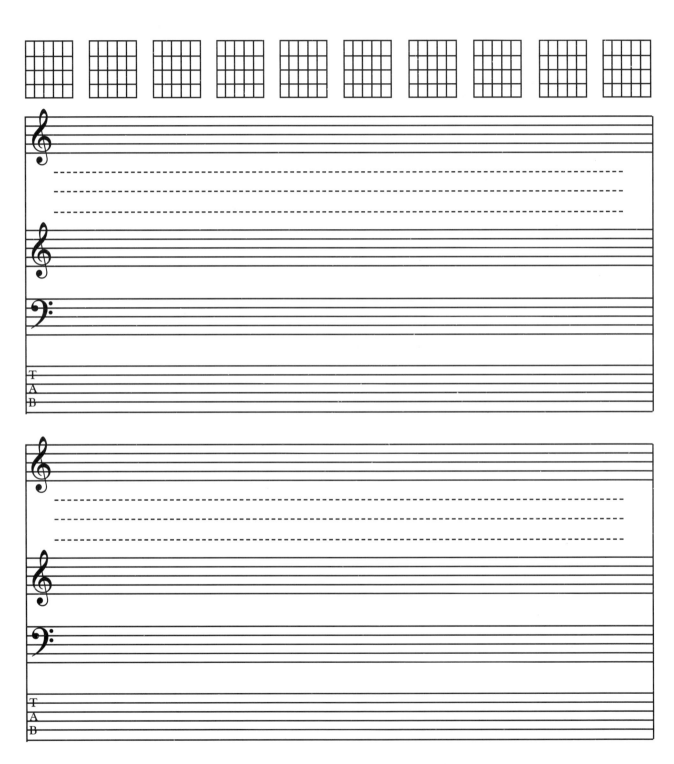

I wait until I get inspired. If your energy is up and your strength is up, then it's a good idea to try to write. I won't touch the piano unless I'm very inspired.

—Brian Wilson (b. 1942), the Beach Boys

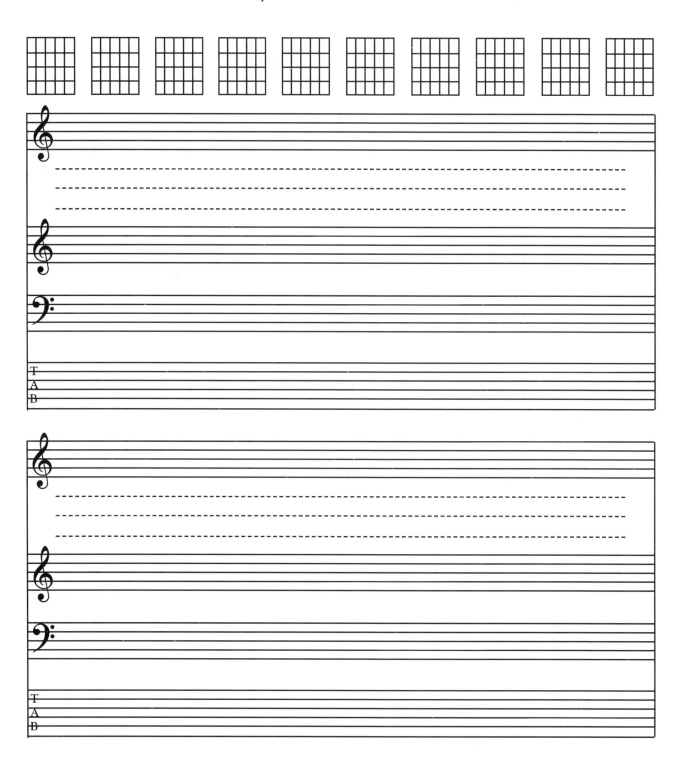

We spent a few months just making music every day and seeing what came out of us. We always try to have our musical output be sincere and just spontaneous—there's nothing calculated about it.

—Adam Levine (b.1979), Maroon 5

People always want to know which part of the song really happened; they want to know some sort of a "Truth." For some reason they can see the same actor acting in 17 different movies, using 17 different hair colors, using fake props, changing their voice, changing their accent, being evil or being the victim, and they are okay with that. They understand that it's just a movie; they understand that it's an art. But with music they forget. Music, somehow, is life.

—Regina Spektor (b. 1980), American musician

I'm trying to write songs; it's hard to write them sometimes. I keep trying to write songs but it rarely happens
…that I finish one. But it's fun to play music and make up stuff and then when it sounds right
I start writing it down and it just turns into a song.

—Daniel Johnston (b. 1961), American musician

After silence, that which comes nearest to expressing the inexpressible
is music.

—Aldous Huxley (1894–1963), English writer

I don't want to be surrounded by computers. I don't want to click and drag to turn up the volume;
I want a console that has a big volume knob on it! The technology to record music is just a necessary evil;
the music is within you.

—Scott McMicken (b. 1978), Dr. Dog

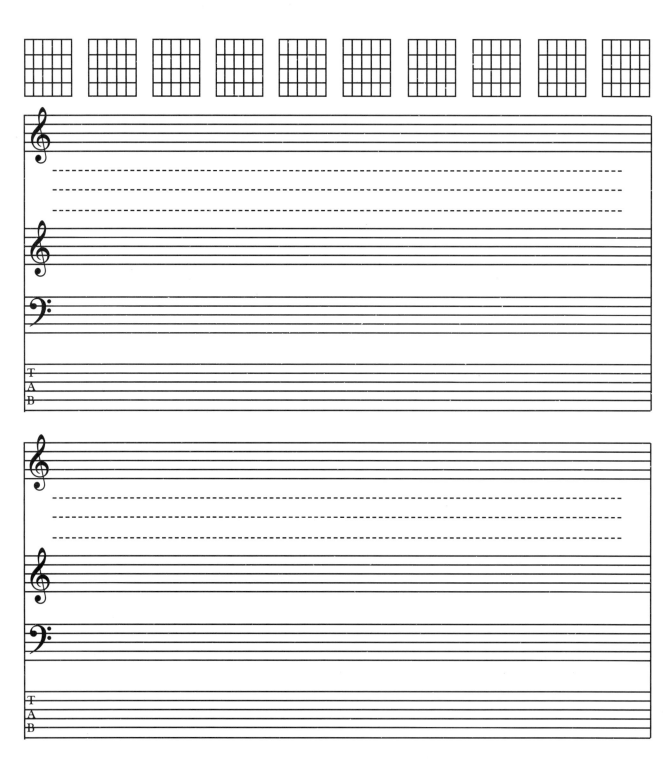

I like to use storytelling and I start with something that's real.

—Guru (1961–2010), Gang Starr

I have a weird life because I live on songwriting royalties, which are a strange income.
Sometimes it rains, sometimes it doesn't.

—Joe Strummer (1952–2002), the Clash

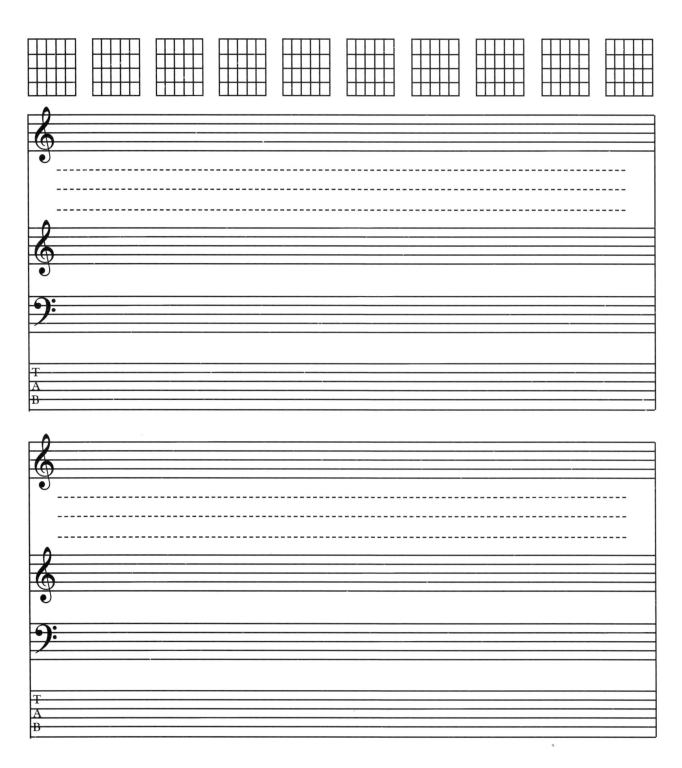

Music is your own experience, your thoughts, your wisdom.
If you don't live it, it won't come out of your horn.

—Charlie Parker (1920–1955), American musician

Those first five or six songs I wrote, I was just taking notes at a fantastic rock concert
that was going on inside my head.

—Jim Morrison (1943–1971), the Doors

I can't really pick what song I like the best or shit like that. It's not that simple to me, man. It's more like a collage of moods.

—Shannon Hoon (1967–1995), Blind Melon

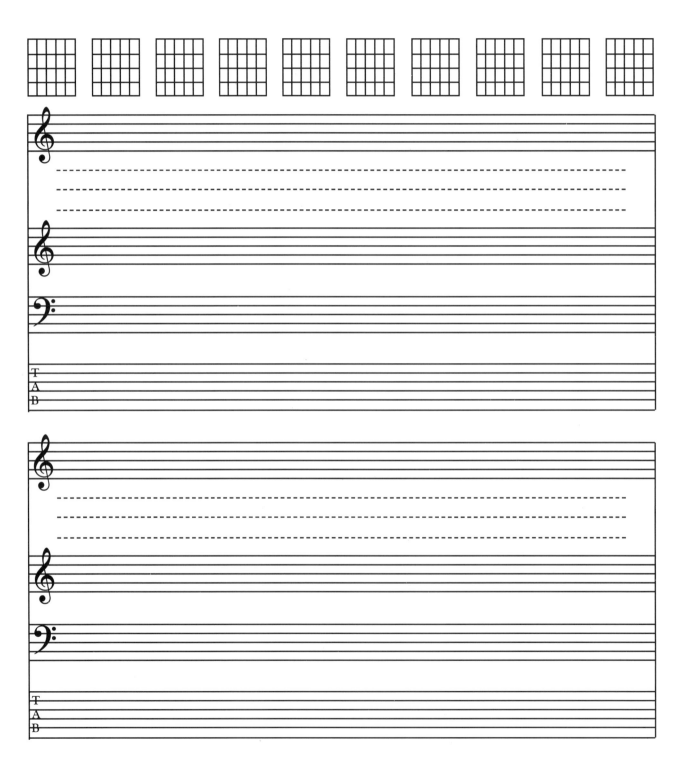

It's a feeling I get when it's right, so I just keep going until I get that feeling. It's like a butterfly type feeling. When I hit it, and it's right, and the mix is right, that's when it's time to come out. Nothing leaves this studio until I get that feeling.

—Dr. Dre (b. 1965), American musician; producer

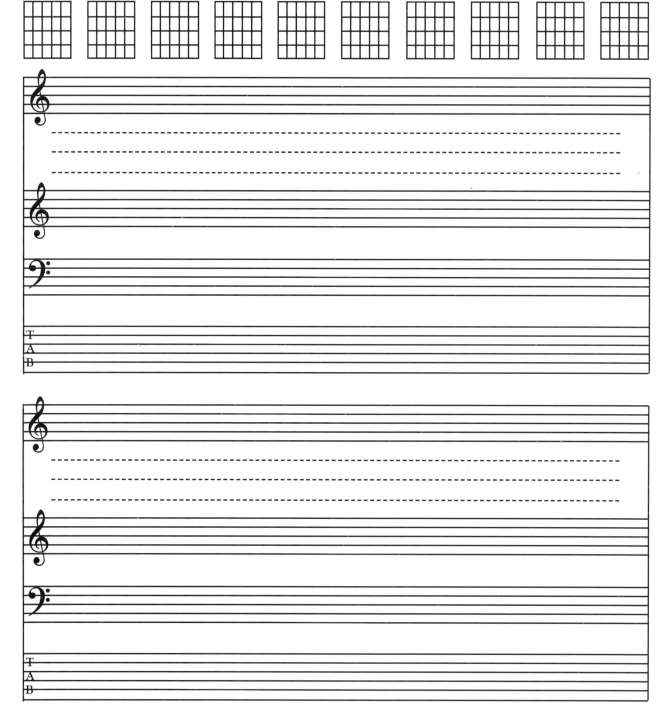

Getting on stage is a bonus, that's my therapy, that's when I can tell stories
and it all makes sense.

—Jason Mraz (b. 1977), American musician

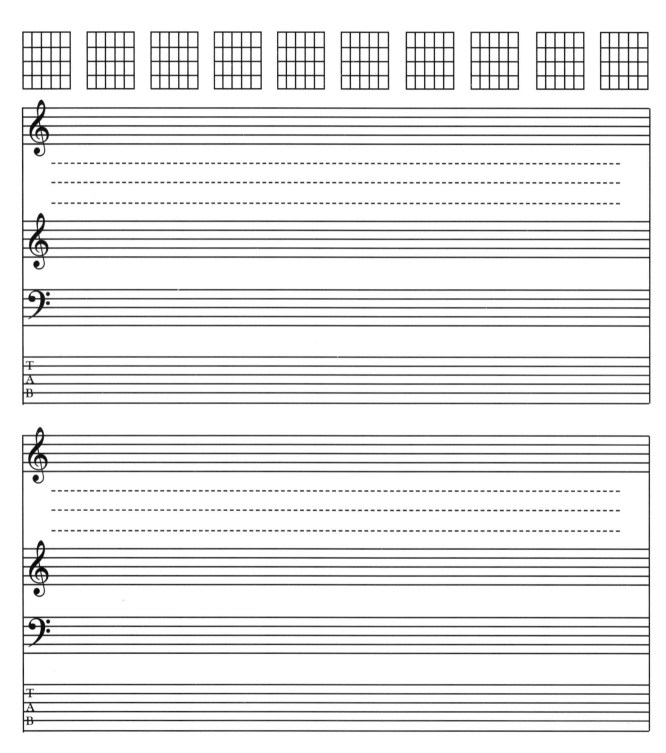

You can do things that have art as its basis that are not in your heart, but are in your soul.

—Phil Spector (b. 1939), American producer; songwriter

I've lived a lifetime of listening to music. When I write songs, it's pulling from bits and pieces of whatever is floating around.

—Mark Foster (b. 1984), Foster the People

In some ways, touring is a restraint on the creative side, because it's hard to write on the road.
So you just have to wait, and sit on this anticipation until the time you're able to spend
days, weeks, months working on something.

—Victoria Legrand (b. 1981), Beach House

I write all the time. You have to experience life, make observations, and ask questions. It's machine-like how things are run now in hip-hop, and my ambitions are different.

—Mos Def (b. 1973), American musician; actor

Being a songwriter, I'm constantly dredging my own self-awareness. To be able to get away from that self-awareness when I go out in public is a nice way to get some distance from myself.

—Ben Gibbard (b. 1976), Death Cab for Cutie; the Postal Service

People want to see a Liberace, they want to see a star. You give 'em a star and they happy; it puts a smile on their face.

—Slick Rick (b. 1965), British-American musician

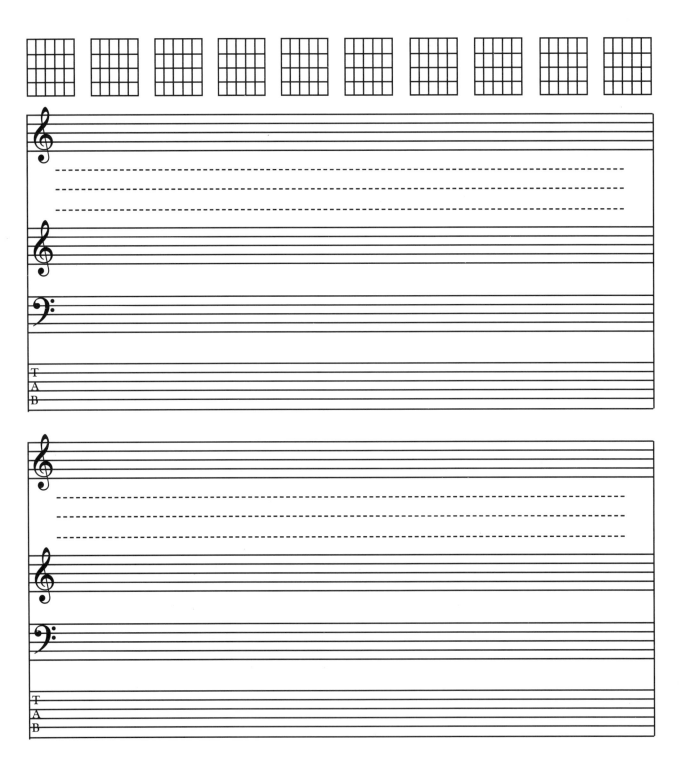

Well, the words for me always come last. And in a certain sense, they do magically come to me, because I really don't know where some of the most memorable lines I've ever written came from. They just come.

—Paul Simon (b. 1941), American musician

The whole point of creating music for me is to give voice to things
that aren't normally given voice to....

—Thom Yorke (b. 1968), Radiohead

The important thing is to feel your music, really feel it and believe it.

Ray Charles (1930-2004), American musician

Without music to decorate it, time is just a bunch of boring production deadlines
or dates by which bills must be paid.

—Frank Zappa (1940–1993), American musician

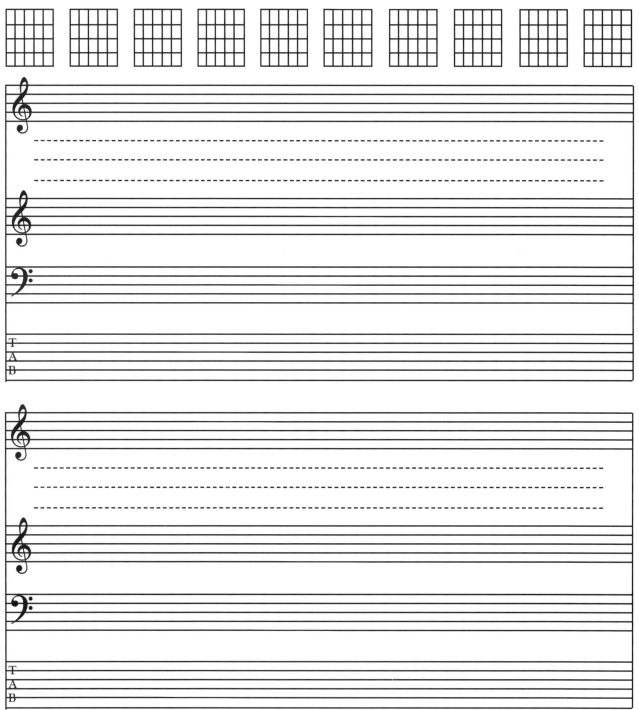

Every time I open my mouth I have to say something
that makes the listener continue listening.

—KRS-One (b. 1965), American musician

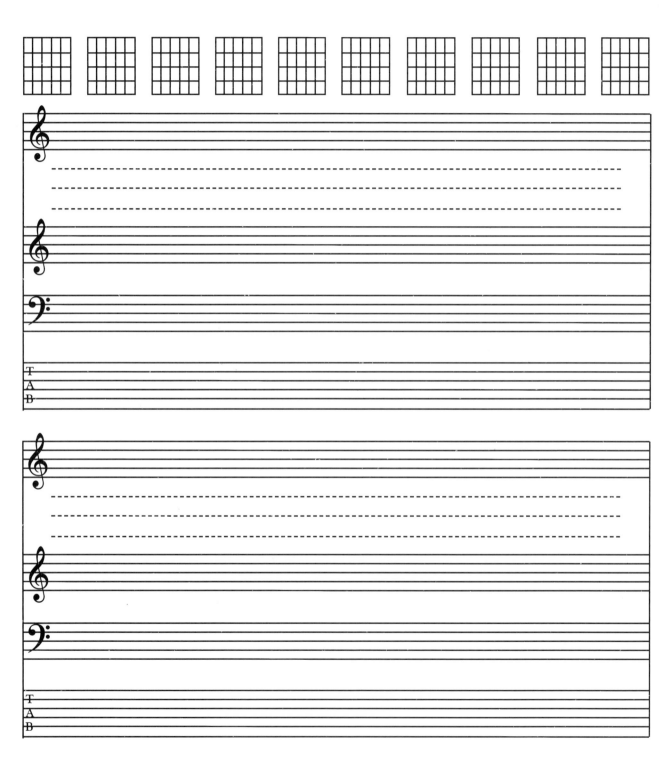

Music can change the world because it can change people.

—Bono (b. 1960), U2

I think we try not to over labor the songs, but we also enjoy taking the time to live with the material.
There have definitely been moments where I thought a song was done only to see it
completely reformed and reshaped.

—Ed Droste (b. 1978), Grizzly Bear

... I also think that it's important for artists to remind their listeners that they're multidimensional, just like the people who listen to them. You're not any one thing. Nobody's linear. We all have many different moods, many different moments in our lives, and we have many different types of behavior.

—Gavin DeGraw (b. 1977), American musician

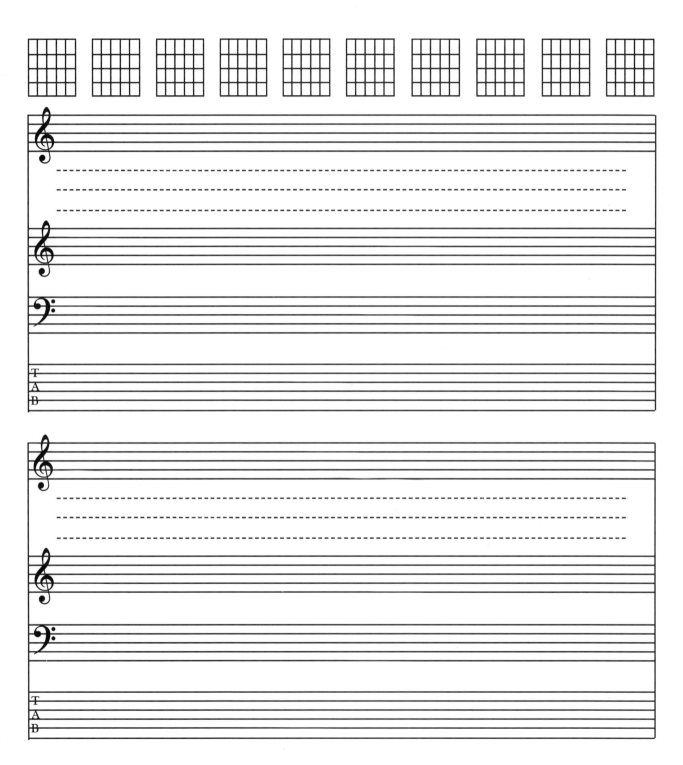

I didn't realize I had a sound but then people started telling me I had a sound in Danger Mouse. It is only after you do things that you realize you have a sound. I realized that with other bands, too. You don't realize you have a sound until after the first record.

—Brian Burton aka Danger Mouse (b. 1977), American producer; musician

All the best songwriting work I do is when my mind isn't working at all.
I like to watch baseball games with a guitar—you don't use your mind at all.

—Peter Buck (b.1956), R.E.M.

Talking about what a song's trying to say is like talking about art.
You know, I think it's in the eye of the beholder and the ear of the listener.

—Roger Daltrey (b. 1944), the Who

When I'm writing songs, I'm just writing songs I like to listen to.
—Eric Earley, Blitzen Trapper

A guitar like Blackie comes along maybe once in a lifetime.
I played it for twelve years non-stop on the road, and it's still got it.

—Eric Clapton (b. 1945), English musician

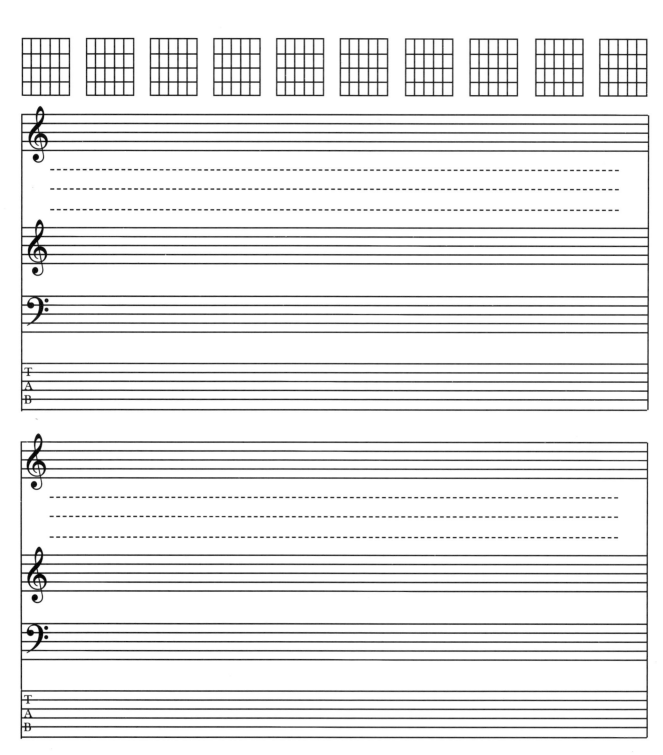

The reason why I collaborate with MCs is that I wanna see if my style can fit with theirs or vice versa. See if we can bring something together.

—Madlib (b. 1973), American musician; producer

All my records—at one time they've been the most important things I've ever done. Even the ones that aren't hits. Even the ones that sell a hundred copies. At one time they've been the most important thing to me.

—Ray Davies (b. 1944), the Kinks

I'd rather be a musician than a rock star.

—George Harrison (1943–2001), the Beatles

Major Chords

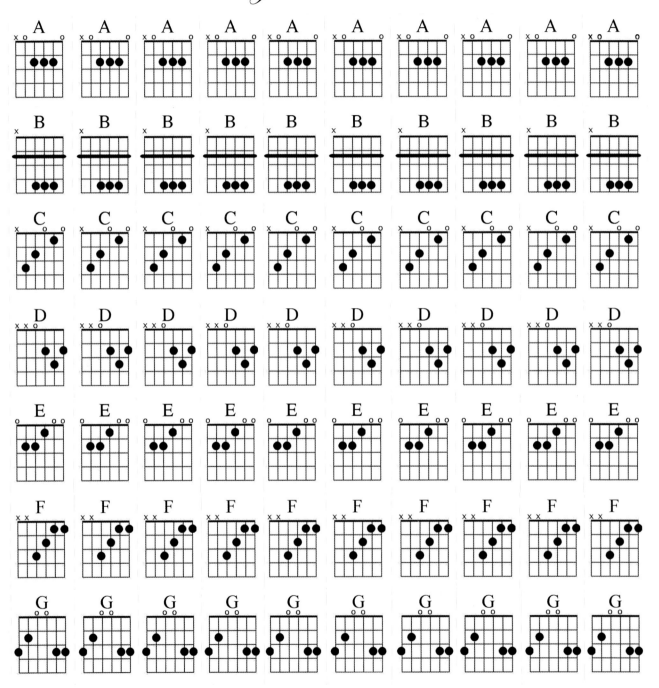

Major Chords

Major Chords

Major Chords

Minor Chords

Minor Chords

Minor Chords

Minor Chords